In Praise of
Libraries

In Praise of
Libraries

New York University Press
Washington Square
New York
1989

Photo credits: All photos in the four-color insert are courtesy of
NYU/Joh Roemer; p. vi, NYU/Fabian Bachrach; pp. xi, xvii, 2, 3, 4,
14, 17, 21, 28, 37, 44, 46, 49, 51, 52, 55, 66, 69, 70, 73, NYU/Phil
Berkun photo; pp. 8, 11, 12, Philippe Couette; pp. 22, 26, 33, cour-
tesy of the British Library; pp. 38, 40, 41, 43, 50, courtesy of the
Collections of the Library of Congress; p. 56, courtesy of the New
York Public Library, Bob Serating; p. 58, 63, courtesy of the New
York Public Library, Anne Day; p. 61, courtesy of the New York
Public Library; pp. 59, 60, 62, 65, 74, courtesy of the New York Public
Library, Peter Aaron, ESTO.

Library of Congress Cataloging-in-Publication Data

Rochell, Carlton C.
   In praise of libraries.
   p. cm.
   ISBN 0-8147-7409-1
       1. Libraries and society.   2. Research libraries.   3. Library
   administrators.   I. Title.
   Z716.4.R6 1989
   020 — dc19   88-3846
                                                                CIP

New York University Press books are printed on acid-free
paper, and their binding materials are chosen
for their strength and durability.

Contents

Introduction

I take great pleasure in introducing this volume. The occasion and inspiration for it was an academic convocation, "In Praise of Libraries and Librarians," held on December 15, 1987, in the atrium of the Elmer Holmes Bobst Library and Study Center at New York University.

At this special convocation, members of the New York University community and our guests paid tribute to six scholar-librarians of international distinction. I was pleased, on behalf of the university, to present the honorary degree of Doctor of Humane Letters to these eminent persons: the Librarian of Congress, James H. Billington; the Librarian of Congress Emeritus, Daniel J. Boorstin; the Director of the Biblioteca Nacional in Spain, Juan Pablo Fusi; the President of the New York Public Library, Vartan Gregorian; the former Administrator General of the Bibliothèque Nationale in France, André Miguel; and the Chairman of the British Library, Lord Anthony Meredith Quinton.

The appearance of this volume, based on the proceedings of that event, represents a proud moment for New York University, the institution I am privileged to serve, and for me. When I was a Member of Congress, one of the areas of legislation in which I took a particular interest was libraries, and during my years in the House of Representatives, I helped write a number of measures to assist public libraries; grade school and high school libraries; college, university, and research libraries; and the Library of Congress.

▼ ▼ ▼

I am sure that the distinguished heads of the great libraries represented in these pages agree that libraries are indispensable to a genuinely free and creative society and that no society that fails to support them can pretend to be civilized. Indeed, as Barbara Tuchman has said, "Books are the carriers of civilization. Without books, history is silent, literature dumb, science crippled, thought and speculation at a standstill."

In a university community, of course, a library is more than a building containing books; it is an engine of the academic enterprise, vital to the central purpose of sharing and advancing knowledge. At New York University, under the outstanding direction of Dean Carlton Rochell, the Bobst Library has become a leader in the areas of resource sharing, preservation programs, special collections, and the use of computer technology.

Nevertheless, like most libraries today, our magnificent library faces an array of challenges. Nearly every research library in the United States—in the world!—is caught by the pressures of increasing demands, rapidly changing technology, and inadequate financial support.

Obviously, in order effectively to serve the needs of students and teachers, research libraries must expand. Yet, the books and periodicals required for expansion have become more and more costly. Moreover, as library holdings grow, so do problems of preservation. Nearly eighty percent of the books and artifacts in American libraries are threatened by aging.

Beyond coping with such problems as these, libraries today, both to survive and to serve the burgeoning needs of society, must modernize, economize, and share technologies. Although the idea of building linkages among libraries is not novel, during the last decade the concept of networks—for access, collection development and preservation—has taken hold and spread throughout the country and the world.

In this connection, I am pleased that New York University is a member of the Research Libraries Group, a consortium of 36 universities and other research institutions in the United States, and proud that Dean Rochell is now serving as Chairman of the Board of this prestigious organization. Together, the Research Libraries Information Network (RLIN), the On-line Computer Library Center (OCLC), and the Western Library Network provide bibliographic information on more than 25 million books, periodicals, maps, audiovisual holdings, and other materials.

Libraries and Librarians today, whether in the United States, Britain, France, or Spain, are operating on the frontiers of automation and technology. Yet complex as the new library world has become, libraries remain fundamentally about readers, writers, and books.

In this respect, two qualities are common to the distinguished persons whom we honor in this volume. First, of course, is that each either leads or has led one of the most important research libraries in the world. Second, all six are scholars. They not only read and study books; they write them. Here Daniel Boorstin reminds us that in a 1939 letter to President Franklin D. Roosevelt, his friend, Supreme Court Justice Felix Frankfurter, advised FDR to choose as Librarian of Congress someone who "knows books, loves books and makes books." What a fitting description of all our six honorees!

I must express my gratitude for the generosity of several persons who helped make possible the publication of this book. The first is a member of the New York University Board of Trustees who also chairs its important Committee for the Year 2000, charged with planning the future of the university, Mrs. Marie Schwartz. Her name and that of her late husband, Arnold Schwartz, grace many buildings and programs at NYU and reflect thereby the wide range of their concerns—from health care to the arts to better understanding of how public

▼ ▼ ▼

policy is formed in the United States. This publication was underwritten by a grant from the Arnold and Marie Schwartz Fund for Education and Health Research.

The second, also a member of the New York University Board of Trustees, is Honorary Curator of the Elmer Holmes Bobst Library and Study Center. Because of the great generosity of her late husband, and her own, the name "Bobst" has become synonymous with a love of learning and libraries. We at New York University are deeply in the debt of Mr. and Mrs. Bobst. The library they made possible is not only a major center of scholarship, but the anchor of the entire university.

Finally, I should like warmly to thank the men and women who work to win support for our library, the "Friends of Bobst Library," as well as all those who serve on the faculty and staff of the library.

This book reflects the most respected thought on libraries today. I hope it will not only attract the attention of librarians and scholars, but will move others to discover for themselves the treasures of the mind and the imagination to which libraries are home.

John Brademas
President, New York University

x

Mrs. Elmer H. Bobst and NYU President John Brademas

Mrs. Bobst addresses the convocation guests and audience

Foreword

The role of libraries in our lives as scholars is a crucial one, and the role of New York University's library, no less so. Bobst Library changed the face of New York University. This structure is symbolic of our mission: to take our place among the foremost research institutions of this nation. In acknowledging the crucial role of this library in the transformation of the university, I speak by inference of the critical role all libraries play, not only in the world of academe, but in our culture.

The founding and support of libraries is really the celebration of the power of the word, the *logos*, amongst us. My youth was punctuated each week by the prologue to the Gospel According to St. John. There the power of the word is identified with the essential power of all creation. I thought it was appropriate at least once today for the sonorous sound of Latin to be heard. *"In principio erat verbum, et verbum erat apud deum, et Deus erat verbum. Hoc erat in principio apud deum. Omnia per ipsum facta sunt, et sine ipso factum est nihil, quod factum est: in ipso vita erat, et vita erat lux hominum, et lux in tenebris lucet."*

"In the beginning was the Word. And the Word was with God and the Word was God, and the same was in the beginning with God, all things were made according to the Word, and without it was made nothing that was made. And it was Life, and the life was the light of the world, and the light shineth in the darkness."

And so we of New York University gather to recognize our honorees, who have given faithful service to this sacred calling: the release of creativity on behalf of humankind.

L. Jay Oliva
Chancellor and Executive Vice President for Academic Affairs
New York University

xiii

Preface

New York University's special academic convocation, "In Praise of Libraries," was indeed "special." Unlike most library conferences, meetings, workshops, and seminars these days, the NYU convocation focused not on the needs, problems, or failings of libraries, but on their accomplishments, their value, and their importance to daily life.

In his remarks, Juan Pablo Fusi, director of Spain's Biblioteca Nacional, reminded us that Victor Hugo had called libraries "an act of faith." In many ways, the convocation was a celebration of that faith, convened by an academic leader whose commitment to libraries has been a powerful influence throughout his career. Both in Congress and in the academic community, New York University's President John Brademas has unfailingly championed the cause of libraries — and libraries that serve the general public as well as those that serve scholarship and university communities.

In honoring the scholars who lead or have led today's great libraries, we honored principles of stewardship as old as the most ancient clay tablet and as modern as the newest microchip. We recognized librarians as the stewards of humanity's intellectual heritage. Yet, while acknowledging the unchanging mission of libraries, convocation speakers did not ignore the challenges that confront them today.

The information explosion, the enormous increase in scholarly output, was raised by Vartan Gregorian, president of the New York Public Library. Reminding us that "the amount of available information doubles every five years," he pointed

▼ ▼ ▼

out that "the ratio of used to available information is decreasing all the time."

There can be no more vivid example of the library storage dilemma than was offered by James H. Billington, Librarian of Congress. "Nearly three-fourths of the books in the Library of Congress," he reported, "are in foreign languages that Americans have generally ceased to study."

Urging greater international cooperation in the preservation of library materials, André Miguel, former administrator general of France's Bibliothèque Nationale, added a poignant appeal to involve writers and editors in conservation efforts. Noting that "the dream of the writer . . . is a dream of eternity," he asked, "What is a book for eternity if it is mortal, like him . . . destined to dust?"

Acknowledgment of library problems, however, in no way diminished recognition of library virtues. There emerged, as a dominant theme of the convocation, an image of the library as a unique educational setting, site of the purest kind of learning — independent inquiry — where the individual encounters knowledge face-to-face, with no intermediaries, no prerequisites, no restrictions, no need to justify access, and no examinations to pass.

Dr. Gregorian called his library, "Everyman's university." Lord Quinton, chairman of the British Library, stressing the obligations of a national library to layreaders, recalled how Martin Luther had proclaimed the priesthood of all believers. "What I am arguing for," he said, "is a kind of Lutheranism of scholarship," noting that "many readers who are not scholars in the strictest sense have a potentially scholarly interest in something."

Freedom of inquiry was equated throughout with political freedom, and access to information with personal freedom. Daniel J. Boorstin, Librarian of Congress Emeritus, put it best when he referred to "the mystery and the paradox of freedom, of which libraries are the symbol."

Carlton C. Rochell
Dean of Libraries, New York University

Lord Anthony Quinton during the convocation ceremony.

In Praise of
Libraries

Juan Pablo Fusi
—on the—
Biblioteca Nacional

The Biblioteca Nacional

In 1711, King Philip V agreed to the creation of a Royal Library in Madrid. The library opened in March 1712, and remained a royal institution until 1836, when the State took it over and renamed it the Biblioteca Nacional. To assist in the formation of the library, the King gave approximately 8,000 books, manuscripts, and prints, as well as coins, medals, and other antiquities. In 1716, King Philip decreed that one copy of everything printed in Spain had to be deposited in the Royal Library. By 1874, the libraries collection had grown to 300,000 books;

1

by 1934, it was almost 1,500,000 volumes; by 1988, more than 4,000,000, including 26,122 of manuscripts, 3,000 incunabula, 48,000 rare books, prints, music, maps, and reviews.

Although the library's resources were equal to those of other European national libraries, they were not very accessible to scholars. A movement for reform, which began in the early nineteenth century, culminated in the royal decree of May 15, 1930, which stated that the objects of the Biblioteca Nacional were to acquire books, to inspect the internal organization of the library, to promote cooperation with other libraries both domestic and foreign, to encourage gifts and

Dr. Juan Pablo Fusi, Director of the Biblioteca Nacional, Spain

Dr. Juan Pablo Fusi and Professor André Miguel

legacies from individuals and corporations, to organize exhibitions and conferences, and to prepare catalogues. As a result of this decree, the library expanded its hours, separated students and scholars from general readers, published catalogues, and expanded acquisitions and exchange programs.

Originally, the library was housed in the Royal Palace, but it was moved during the French occupation of Bonaparte. The present building was begun in 1866 and was not completed until 1894.

Presentation to Dr. Juan Pablo Fusi

Convocation remarks by Dr. Juan Pablo Fusi

▼ ▼ ▼

PRESENTATION TO JUAN PABLO FUSI
by President John Brademas

Juan Pablo Fusi—historian and scholar, your studies of the transition of Spain from dictatorship to democracy and your biography of Franco have won you wide praise. Said no less an authority than the great interpreter of the Spanish labyrinth, Gerald Brenan, of your work: ". . . Great care has been taken to deliver the truth . . ." You have held several distinguished academic positions in your country and abroad, including heading the Iberian Center at St. Anthony's College, Oxford. Since 1985, you have been director of the Biblioteca Nacional in Madrid. On assuming your post as leader of the most important library in the Hispanic world, you moved vigorously to redefine the library's role. Inspired by the proverb, "El saber ocupa lugar"—"Knowledge takes up space"—you have asserted that the Biblioteca Nacional must serve two purposes: at once a center of research and the axis of the nation's library system. You have worked both to preserve great treasures of Spain's glorious past and, by enlarging and modernizing, to bring the library into the twentieth century.

Juan Pablo Fusi—you have taken seriously the exhortation of your countryman, Ortega y Gasset: Without a National Library, Spain will be disgraced. You are determined that the libraries of Spain will do honor to the proud tradition of the Spanish people. By virtue of the authority vested in me, I am pleased to confer upon you, the Degree of Doctor of Humane Letters, honoris causa.

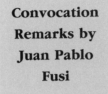

Convocation Remarks by Juan Pablo Fusi

The celebrated Argentinian writer, Jorge Luis Borges, Director of the Buenos Aires National Library for almost twenty years from 1955 to 1974, wrote: "There are people who cannot imagine a world without birds. There are people who cannot imagine a world without water. As for myself, I am unable to imagine a world without books."

It is, therefore, no wonder that Borges, after he became blind, imagined Paradise in the form of a library in his sad "Poema de los Dones" ("Poem of the Gifts"). I agree with the first part of his proposition — the modern world is inconceivable without books. But I am not sure that I agree with the second part — with the image of libraries as Paradise. At least six out of seven days a week, I find myself thinking that the library, at least the Spanish library, is truly not Paradise, but Hell. Only on Sundays, perhaps because in my own language it means "the Day of the Lord" and under the Lord's inspiration I think like Borges, do I think that the library is Paradise. But it is a short-lived illusion. It lasts me exactly until early Monday morning. From Monday until Saturday, I think not like Borges, but rather like Victor Hugo, that all libraries are an act of faith. The faith needed to face the intimidating difficulties, vast amounts of work, inadequate budgets and personnel, and faith, too, to believe that modern man still retains some need, or passion for, or just pleasure in, books, which, once again in Borges' words, "hold time magically dried up and preserved." I do not know where all of this faith arises from; perhaps it might be that we believe, however unconsciously, as the Spanish philosopher Ortega y Gasset once wrote, that democratic societies are the offsprings of books; and we might add, of libraries.

Faith by itself will move mountains, or so people say, but faith alone does not make libraries. Libraries are the work of librarians. With excellent judgment, the Dictionary of Author-

▼ ▼ ▼

ities of the Spanish Royal Academy, published in 1726, wrote about the job of librarian: "It is a job of high esteem and trust, that demands great knowledge and doctrine." Because of this reason, Philip the Fifth, founded the Spanish National Library in 1716, placed a Jesuit at the head of the library, and named him his Royal Confessor—a position that, since the monarchy has now been restored, would not displease me at all to recover.

Things have changed since 1726. Librarians have gained in knowledge and doctrine. But I doubt whether they have gained in esteem. Indeed, I think society, at least Spanish society, does not fully value the services rendered to it by the librarians. But, librarians do form an essential part in the bibliographical education of countries. Librarians, as Ortega put it in 1935, act as filters in between the floor of books and the reader; and librarians are, as well, historians of the book, and as such, historians of intellectual life and culture.

And it is for these reasons that I value the initiative of New York University so highly; for these reasons I have accepted the honor granted to me. Unlike my distinguished colleagues, my presence here is not due to personal merits, which, at my age, by definition are almost none. As a historian, not everything I wrote is bad, but I have only excelled in my choice of mentors, whom I would like to mention here: Sir Raymond Carr and Dr. Joachim Romero Maura. I am here on behalf of all those who have made the Spanish National Library, on behalf of all the people who now work in it, and on behalf of their predecessors and mine, which are a rather peculiar lot, which includes, even, one General Inquisitor. In their name, and in mine, thank you very much.

André Miguel
——*on the*——
Bibliothèque Nationale

The Bibliothèque Nationale

Located in the heart of Paris, the Bibliothèque Nationale, one of the high points of the intellectual life of France, and one of its most prestigious symbols, contains approximately 12,000,000 books, 500,000 periodicals defunct or current, 650,000 maps and plans, 15,000,000 prints, photographs, engravings, and posters, 180,000 manuscripts, 800,000 coins, medals, and ancient objects, 2,000,000 scores and other musical documents, 900,000 soundtracks and au-

The Main Reading Room of Bibliothèque Nationale, with its audacious composition of vaults and cupolas

▼ ▼ ▼

diovisual documents, 3,000,000 documents relating to art and the history of the performing arts. To these one should add the Bibliothèque de l'Arsenal, which holds 1,100,000 printed documents, manuscripts, and prints. Equally part of the Bibliothèque Nationale are the annex at Versailles, the library/museum at the Opera, the library of the Conservatoire National de Musique, the Maison Jean Vilar in Avignon, the Center for preservation of periodicals at Provins, and the Center for Book Preservation at Sable. For each of these specialized departments, the Bibliothèque Nationale has a consulting center. Finally, various specialized departments and services complete this array: Access offices (for French and foreign users), centers for the coordination of bibliographic and technical services, automation, restoration, photography, loans, exhibits, press services, hospitality, commercial services, legal services, archives. Three permanent museums, not to mention regular exhibits, contribute to show the public the riches of the institution, be they coins and medals, performing arts, or audio materials (Musée Charles Cros).

Such a gathering of national riches could only be the result of a long history. The library was created initially by authority of the kings of France. The first, Charles V, began the royal library in a tower in the Louvre palace in 1368. In 1537, with the edict of Montpellier, François I authorized the right to publish on condition that one copy of every publication be deposited in the King's Library. This had a double purpose: control over all book production as well as the conservation of documents for the "memory of men." With this double vocation was born, what became over the centuries, the legal deposit, a national service entrusted to the Bibliothèque Nationale.

From Fontainebleau where François I had transferred it, the library returned to Paris under the reign of Charles IX. It made extraordinary strides under Louis XIV. The latter showed his great interest in that institution by entrusting it to his greatest ministers, Colbert and Louvois. Colbert trans-

10

A detail of the Main Reading Room, one of the greatest examples of iron architecture

ferred the royal collections to a new site, rue Vivienne, better adapted to their diversity and volume. The growth of the collection led to its first division: printed materials, prints, and manuscripts. Finally, in 1692, the library was opened for the first time to the learned public.

The eighteenth century was another great epoch. The Bibliothèque Nationale settled on its definitive site: the Hôtel de Nevers (remodeled by the architects at Cotte, father and son). They built the wings north and east of the current main courtyard) and the Hôtel de Chivry running along the rue Richelieu. The redistribution of the collection called for a new unit: medals and ancient objects, created in 1741. On October

▼ ▼ ▼

11, 1720, the library was declared officially opened to all scholars.

The revolutionary turmoil, despite the uncertainties which disrupted the administration, was, in the end, beneficial to the Bibliothèque Nationale. Three hundred thousand volumes and manuscripts, confiscated from émigrés and religious congregations, enriched its collection to the point that enlargement and relocation became necessary. The destruction of the existing building and the construction of a new

An overview of the Main Reading Room

▼ ▼ ▼

one, six floors high, was considered. Finally, a long time later, the architect Labrouste was able to undertake a substantial remodeling, but with minimal respect for the architectural past. Of special note is the wing which runs along the rue Richelieu and the main reading room (1868), an audacious composition of vaults and cupolas, one of the greatest examples of iron architecture, and one of the best known areas of the Bibliothèque Nationale.

During the twentieth century, remodeling and extension continued: a second main reading room, for periodicals, called the Oval Room was constructed by the architect Recoura in 1936; the building, and then the extension of the annex at Versailles; the modernization of the areas reserved for maps and prints; the addition of extra stacks for printed materials, the purchase of buildings in the perimeter neighboring the rue Richelieu; the construction, at the corner of that same street and the rue de Louvois, of a building for music and sound archives.

These past years have been marked by various steps taken for long-range planning: the establishment of a plan of protection of the patrimony deposited at the Bibliothèque Nationale; preparations for the automation of catalogues of the collections; the decentralization due to annexes at Provins, Sable, and Avignon; and, finally, in Paris, the inauguration of a new monumental addition along the rue Vivienne. It added 17,000 square meters to the 90,000 which the Bibliothèque Nationale covered in that sector. It permitted three major changes: the relocation of several services that were in tight quarters in the old neighboring buildings; the opening (thanks to the vaulted passage where one can find the shop, the Charles Cros Museum, and the Museum for the Performing Arts) of an auditorium and exhibit halls; and finally, such personnel-related improvements as the restaurant and the child-care center.

Since 1981, the Bibliothèque Nationale, whose staff totals approximately 1,250 individuals, has been part of the Ministry of Culture (Book and Reading Division).

Presentation to Professor André Miguel

Convocation remarks by Professor André Miguel

14

▼▼▼

PRESENTATION TO ANDRÉ MIGUEL
by President John Brademas

André Miguel—scholar, novelist, teacher, librarian, your work on the Islamic world has been described as "a model of humane and penetrating discussion of how one great civilization viewed itself and others." In a series of masterly studies, including your three-volume La géographie humaine du monde musulman, *you have distinguished yourself as one of the preeminent Arabists of our time. In 1984, you accepted the arduous task of administering one of the world's great citadel's of culture, the Bibliothèque Nationale of France. Able to trace its beginnings to 1368, when Charles V began collecting manuscripts in the Old Louvre Palace, the Bibliothèque Nationale today boasts more than 12 million books and 15 million prints and drawings. Mindful of the historic origins of this extraordinary treasure, you remained sensitive to tradition while pressing for administrative reforms and modernization. Attending to the restoration of the Bibliothèque's magnificent building in the heart of Paris, you fought to preserve endangered holdings and to acquire new ones. You have insisted that, in a time of competing demands, support for research libraries is important to the future of France.*

André Miguel—as Administrator General of the Bibliothèque Nationale, you said, "People see it as a silo of books. But they must understand that it is more. It is the memory of our nation." Through your leadership of your nation's library, you helped replenish the reservoir of your nation's memory. I am pleased to confer upon you, by virtue of the authority vested in me, the degree of Doctor of Humane Letters, honoris causa.

▼ ▼ ▼

Convocation Remarks by André Miguel

Thank you very much. I have a secret to confess. But do not repeat it. I am more fluent in French than in English. In 1967, when I defended my thesis for my Doctorate at the Sorbonne, I swore to myself, never again. Yet, here, I am a Doctor for the second time. Wonderfully, without going through the terrible ordeal of being examined, and the defense, after many more or less happy years devoted to work on a book composed for the occasion. Your generosity has spared me the effort.

And I am deeply grateful to you for conferring this honor on me. The only condition imposed was this short speech. Even if I have to deliver the speech in a language I naturally admire, but which never ceases to be a demanding, but never conquered, mistress for me. My emotion today is not only due to the honor bestowed on me, it is all the more intense because it is given to me for the first time in my life in America —and in a city I love passionately. I have always loved New York—even before this love became a slogan and a sticker, a sticker that decorated one of my motorcycles in France.

To tell the truth, perhaps I have come too late. Your intention was aimed at the Director of the Bibliothèque Nationale in France. I am no longer the director, but never mind. It is the institution you want to honor, through me. Libraries in France are confronted with the same problems as libraries all over the world. The destruction of documents due to the poor quality of paper, the rising number of readers, and the growth of collections and attendant storage problems. It is sometimes difficult to convince public authorities that the protection and promotion of culture are just as vital to a nation as its economic health. Furthermore, we know that most of these problems can only be solved at the expense of continual close collaboration between libraries all over the world. Such collaboration includes the interconnection of computerized databases, the coordination of acquisition policies, and regular

▼ ▼ ▼

exchange of information concerning methods for conservation and reproduction. In these three areas, we must develop
international cooperation among libraries.

Perhaps, librarians through the world should also look for
a large-scale information campaign aimed not only at governments, of course, but also at editors and writers, especially
writers. If the editor is mainly interested in the success of a
book, and if the writer naturally follows the editor, the dream
of the writer goes further because it is a dream of eternity. But
of what use is a book for eternity if it is mortal, like its author,
and like its author, destined to dust? Librarians the world over
know this destruction better than everyone else, better than
the writers themselves. So, it is up to librarians to initiate and
develop the alarm.

I should add that as far as my own area of specialization
—the Arabic world and the Third World—is concerned, the

NYU President John Brademas with Dr. Juan Pablo Fusi and Dr.
André Miguel

same cooperation must be developed. Nothing will be done for the future of the world and our children if the world does not learn solidarity. The key words should be greater understanding, and closer cooperation. I take pleasure in thinking that, through the honor you have bestowed on me, you want to underline this fervent obligation.

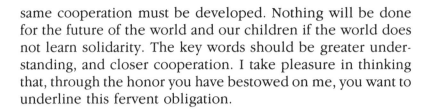

Further Observations by André Miguel

The role, the functions, and what is at stake at the Bibliothèque Nationale elicit, at this very moment, numerous debates and discussions. This statement, therefore, does not express an official point of view; it simply reflects the result of my personal experience, acquired during the last three years and seven months as head of that institution. I must add that I omitted the problems relating strictly to management and administration, as they relate only within the context of France. I shall raise only those questions that deal with the very definition of the Bibliothèque Nationale, as many of those questions are raised in other public libraries, in other countries, and will interest a greater number of people.

In France, whether one wishes it or not, the library is primarily perceived as a private tool. For a long time, the Bibliothèque Nationale remained the personal property of the king. As it turned from royal to national institution, it did not succeed in creating, in the collective conscience, a big movement of imitation. The country—with such notable exceptions as the Sorbonne, Sainte-Genevieve, Strasbourg, and a handful of municipal libraries—did not see the growth, as in other European countries, of a dense network of libraries perfectly equipped and with good services. For the collective conscience, the library remains either the instrument of the

▼ ▼ ▼

researcher who consults the few hundreds, even thousands of books needed, or the pride of the bibliophile, or it stands as a social status of the affluent, cultivated person.

With specific regard to university libraries, the current situation (dramatic in some cases) demonstrates the absence, in the past as well as the present, of a coherent and determined policy. One must never forget in the case of the Bibliothèque Nationale that, contrary to its British counterpart which is freed of many tasks because of its proximity to two powerful neighbors, Oxford and Cambridge, the Bibliothèque Nationale takes upon itself, for Paris and even for the whole of France, the task of serving researchers as a classic research library on a daily basis. It is thus frequently consulted and must bear daily the pressure of a large number of users: the main reading room for printed materials, which has 376 seats, sometimes accommodates on a daily basis double that number of visitors and, even a thousand users during the summer months. It is thus in contrast with what ought to be a coherent and serviceable system of libraries in the whole of France that one should judge the ideal role of the Bibliothèque Nationale.

The reader at the Bibliothèque Nationale should be—with no reference to social status, but to academic status—a researcher, by profession, by vocation, or by circumstance, who comes to the Bibliothèque Nationale to find either a rare document (unknown, lost, or forgotten) or else a set of documents of various types that could be found elsewhere but which only the Bibliothèque Nationale can provide in one visit.

As an aside, because of the richness and diversity of the collections, one can note a fundamental phenomenon. Created in a disorganized manner, with disparate documents—books, manuscripts, maps, prints, medals, records—the Bibliothèque Nationale has become, at the time of multidisciplines and multidocumentation, the very tool of research in our times. Hence the need to keep that tool as is, in the richness of its components which make the Bibliothèque Na-

19

tionale not only a library, but a conservatory of the patrimony of the nation, of its memory, a "mnemotheque."

Thus the Bibliothèque Nationale differs from a classical research library, particularly from an academic library, and even from a public library. If communication is the function bestowed on the Bibliothèque Nationale as on any other, that function must, in view of its very definition, relate to a document that the Bibliothèque Nationale must conserve. The legal deposit, on which it depends, has no other goal than to keep all that is published so as to ensure for future generations the presence of an item, at least of a document which would have otherwise disappeared. But this double function of conservation and communication of rare documents matches a third function: reproduction, which permits the other two by preserving the original by making its contents available. I do not think that this triple problem does not arise in other similar institutions, but in France it presents itself in a particular fashion in view of the whole library-economical context.

All of this concerns the researcher. But a national library, even though located in the capital city, must indeed not forget its name; those in the nation who contribute to its upkeep have the right to know what it does. Yes, they have the right to see exhibited a few of those pieces that compose this national treasure. They can also require that it make a profit from its collections to match the efforts of the State by the sale of printed books, reproductions, photocopies, photographs, and the commercialization of databases. They can also expect private funding: an example is the release of the videodisc on the French Revolution that was made possible by contributions from an important foreign group, which was not only valuable in itself but because it created a precedent so that in France and abroad one can gain an awareness of the stakes: national memory, as I was saying just now, but also the memory of humanity.

An overview of convocation ceremony

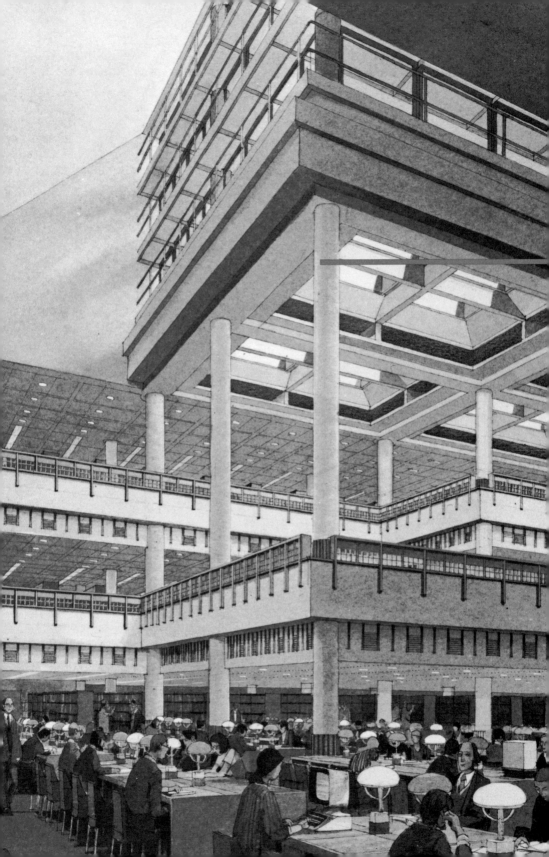

Lord Anthony Meredith Quinton
on the
British Library

The British Library[1]

The British Library, established by Act of Parliament in 1973, has three main divisions: Humanities and Social Sciences; Science, Technology and Industry; and Bibliographic Services. There are also a Research and Development Department and a Central Administration.

Humanities and Social Sciences is the part the public is most familiar with, for it was formed in the main from the library departments of the British Museum—that is, the Department of

---

[1]Extract from *The Reference Division Collections.*
© 1983 The British Library Board

An artist's impression of the Humanities Reading Room at the British Library

Printed Books, the Department of Manuscripts, the Department of Oriental Printed Books and Manuscripts, and the National Reference Library for Science and Invention (now the Science Reference Library). The holdings of these departments, which today number more than 10 million volumes, began as three collections of manuscripts, books, and other material whose acquisition by the state in the eighteenth century led directly to the establishment of the British Museum by the British Museum Act of 1753. The 1753 Act provided for the safe preservation of three collections in the care of a Board of Trustees "for publick use to all Posterity"—a phrase which neatly encapsulates the main aims and functions of today's library.

The three foundation collections of books and manuscripts in the British Museum's Library department were all made by individual collectors. Foremost among them, because it was the bequeathing of his collections to the nation which was the spur to the establishment of the British Museum, was Sir Hans Sloane.

This physician, amateur scientist, antiquarian, and President of the Royal Society built up collections of natural history, geological, zoological and medical phenomena, antiquities from Greece, Rome, Egypt, and the Orient, drawings, coins and medals, and many books and manuscripts whose value and importance were recognized in his own lifetime.

The government accepted the bequest, deciding to house it with another state-owned collection, the Cotton collection of medieval manuscripts, cartularies, state papers and antiquities, whose importance may be judged from the fact that it counted among its treasures the Lindisfarne Gospels, two copies of Magna Carta, and the manuscript of Beowulf. This collection was made by Sir Robert Cotton during the reigns of Elizabeth I and James I.

At the same time, the government also bought the Harleian collection of manuscripts, charters and rolls made by

▼ ▼ ▼

Robert Harley, first Earl of Oxford and one-time chief minister to Queen Anne, and his son, Edward, the second Earl.

By the time the British Museum, housed in Montague House, a former ducal mansion in Bloomsbury, opened in 1759, a fourth important collection had been added to the first three. This was the old Royal Library (so-called to distinguish it from the library collected by George III, most of which also found its way into the British Museum), which was begun in the 1470s by Edward IV, added to by succeeding monarchs, and given to the Museum by George II in 1757.

This magnificent gift brought to the Museum thousands of manuscripts and printed books, including such items as the fifth-century Greek biblical manuscript, the Codex Alexandrinus. It also brought the museum the important right of copyright deposit, under the Act of 1709 which had provided that the Royal Library should receive one copy of every printed work registered at Stationers' Hall.

Services for readers, who were comparatively few until the early nineteenth century, developed steadily. The Reading Room was moved several times, the present round and domed Reading Room, which was opened in 1857, being the Museum's seventh.

Under reforms initiated by Antonio Panizzi (later Sir Anthony Panizzi), Keeper of Printed Books from 1837 and Principal Librarian from 1856 to 1866, the Museum was transformed into a great cultural repository and the library departments became in fact, if not yet in name, the national library of Britain.

Specialist collections, such as those of maps, music, and official papers, grew rapidly in the second half of the nineteenth century, and public exhibitions of items from the library collections became a permanent feature of the Grenville and King's Libraries. Firm implementation of the 1842 Copyright Act also meant that printed material now came into the British Museum's library departments in enormous quantities

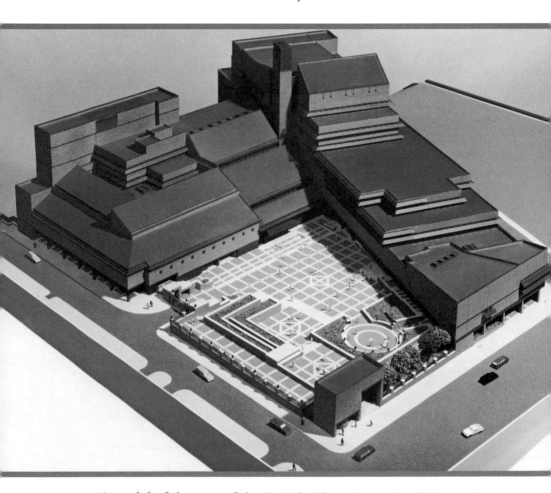

A model of the part of the British Library's new building under construction

from Great Britain, while the expansion of Empire brought even more material from all parts of the world. All this material was housed on the Bloomsbury site.

An important advance in the quality of the service the library departments offered their readers was the publication

▼ ▼ ▼

of a printed catalogue during the latter part of the nineteenth century. Before this, the General Catalogue was available only in unwieldy manuscript form. A Subject Index was also used. All this is now being computerized.

The twentieth century has seen continuing growth. In 1960 the British Museum was given responsibility for creating the National Reference Library for Science and Invention by taking over and expanding the Patent Office Library, one of the country's leading science and technology libraries founded in 1855. The most far-reaching development of recent years has been the establishment of the national British Library, in which the former library departments of the museum make up the major part of the departments of Humanities and Social Sciences. In 1982 responsibility for the admission of the India Office Library and Records was transferred from the Foreign and Commonwealth Office to the Board of the British Library.

Although the library has otherwise entirely severed its two centuries-long connection with the museum, it still has its main home in the Bloomsbury building and is likely to continue to occupy parts of it until its own building in Euston Road just west of St Pancras Station is ready for occupation.

At the moment the British Library occupies some eighteen sites in London—for use by readers, for storage, for administration, for research and development—and there is a large complex at Boston Spa in Yorkshire which houses the Library's Document Supply Centre and employs 750 of the 2,500 people who work for the library. The aim is to bring nearly all the parts of the library that are in London together on a single site. The first stage of the work at St Pancras is well advanced. It is hoped to open some services to readers there by 1993.

Presentation to Lord Anthony Quinton

Convocation remarks by Lord Anthony Quinton

▼ ▼ ▼

PRESENTATION TO LORD ANTHONY MEREDITH QUINTON
by President John Brademas

Lord Anthony Meredith Quinton — chairman of The British Library; former president of Trinity College, Oxford; philosopher and historian of ideas, you are a luminous star in the constellation of British intellectual life. In a range of publications — The Nature of Things, Utilitarian Ethics, The Politics of Imperfection, *and* Thoughts and Thinkers *— you uncover the links between philosophy and science, literature, art, and religion. Graduate of Oxford, where you were a Christ Church man, with first class honors; fellow of all Souls and of New College; you served for eight years as head of Trinity College. A skilled administrator as well as accomplished scholar, you were created a life peer in 1982 and, in 1985, chosen to lead the national library of the United Kingdom. In* The International Who's Who, *under "Leisure interests" you listed "sedentary pursuits." As it undertakes its most ambitious program of rebuilding and reorganizing, The British Library is fortunate to have as its chairman a person whose mind and imagination are anything but sedentary.*

Lord Anthony Meredith Quinton — my own first tutor at Oxford, you have been described — I can say accurately — as "a natural instructor," one who can make "the difficult clear, the obscure palpable, and the fantastic even plausible. . . ." In your many visits to the United States, including to Washington Square, your warmth, wit, and vivacious intelligence have won you many friends and admirers. I take much personal pleasure in conferring upon you, by virtue of the authority vested in me, the degree of Doctor of Humane Letters, honoris causa.

▼ ▼ ▼

Convocation Remarks by Lord Anthony Meredith Quinton

I very much enjoyed hearing what has just been said behind my back by way of citation. I do not expect I have ever been spoken about so agreeably both in those remarks and then, shortly afterwards, John, by you. I realized, when I received the information about the order of events this afternoon at the convocation, that the inexorable cruelty of alphabetical order would place me at the end of the speakers. I meditated a change of names to "Aaronson," but I did not know the legal arrangements over here required to bring about this helpful effect and it was no use congratulating myself that I was not called Zymierski, as it would have made no difference today. I was naturally rather worried, lest anything I had to say would be said by my admired fellow honorands before my turn came.

I have been greatly impressed by the things they have said, but I am delighted they did not use my quotation. For I, too, have one. It is from Thomas Carlyle, who said (and I think it is probably best, in the interests of general intelligibility, that I do not essay a Scottish accent), "The true university, at the present time, is a collection of books." The present time he was speaking of, I imagine, was the 1830s, but it was a kind of brilliant prospective idea of the Bobst Library. Here, after all, is the nerve center of this great university which it has been my happiness, through friendship with John Brademas, to visit on a number of occasions: and I think it is magnificent that right at the top of the library is the point from which he looks out over this vast, diverse, and admirable institution.

The emblem which you have invoked to honor us today, was "In Praise of Libraries and Librarians." And as I say, mindful of my terminal position in the oratorical sequence today, I thought I had better do what is called in England "taking a long run." That is to say, reflect for a moment on libraries in general and on the largest possible scale. On the whole, if I

30

▼ ▼ ▼

may compress primate history into a few sentences, what raises us above the other animals, insofar as we are above them (and I think it would be unduly self-effacing of us to deny that in many respects we are ahead of them; to start with they are all largely afraid of us) is that we have language.

That, of course, was an enormous evolutionary leap; the achievement of a genuine language, and not just the minimal signalling system, which is the most that the other animals have risen to. Then, later on, much nearer our own time, when our species had been in existence for a considerable time, we found out how to embalm language in writing. But best of all was the discovery of alphabetic writing, with its extraordinary flexibility, despite such slightly painful consequences as the alphabet sometimes has to those, such as convocation speakers, who use it.

Now writing was the beginning of something very important. But writing is no use or at any rate its enormous and fantastic potential is not realized until writing is preserved. The immediate note which reminds one to buy two sugar-free Jellos, or, alternatively, the brisk communication "Are you free for dinner after this?" are not kept, or, at any rate, one hopes they are not kept. But, once matter of lasting significance, original thoughts, are put into writing, then it is proper to keep them. And that, really, is what differentiates civilized man from noncivilized man. You might well say it is a slightly absurd consequence of what I have said that Homer was not a civilized man. It is a feat that few could master, to remember (let alone compose, always supposing it had a single composer) a poetic work of sublime merit at that enormous length. We do not need to do this; our libraries will do it for us, in the words of Count Axel, appropriately adjusted.

So, it is not just that language is a great step forward and writing the next great step forward. It was the collection, the preservation, the rendering permanent of writing that really enabled the vast cooperative bringing together of human discoveries which caused the major advance in the latest epoch

▼ ▼ ▼

of the primate story. And, libraries are of all places, the most comprehensive, most efficient, most ambitious, most deliberate, most determined of all possible accumulators of written matter.

Perhaps writing itself is due for a bit of change. It is one of the problems of being involved in libraries at the present time that people keep coming to you and saying—Do you really need this building? Won't everything be capable of being carried around in a shopping basket? When the third next technological development after compact disc comes along, might you not hold the entire contents of a great library in an Italian poison ring? Already an Encyclopedia can be fitted on to two compact discs. So far they are ideal for checking something, or looking up bibliographical information. But they are still not quite an ideal thing to take out under a tree on a summer's day, as you might do with a volume of poetry.

As an ex-academic, I offer one thought about libraries, a rather grim thought, an intellectual experiment. If one had a choice of having the professors of a country mysteriously carried off by some disease, or having the libraries reduced to dust by a particularly voracious kind of ant, one has painfully to admit that it would be better to preserve the libraries and let the professors go. The professors, who would be of mature years, and with failing memories, would not recall all that much of the accumulated civilized tradition it is their business to expound. Professors, in a way, are buckets: they go to the library and, being slightly leaky buckets carry only a part of its contents to the students who are going to benefit from it. But that content is all there in the libraries for new generations, Carlyle's fashion, to find for themselves.

That leads me to my final thought, which is that it is not embarrassing, as I think Dr. Billington was the first to say, for us to come up and be the bearers, the happy and grateful bearers, of the honor you have done to us today in giving us these degrees. We are honored as librarians, because we are not really librarians proper at all; we are more or less decorative objects affixed to the top of great bodies of extremely professional librarians. All of us, I think, got into the library business, if I may so describe it, through the academic route. So my grim experiment has a certain poignancy for us. But not being a true librarian, I can quite decently praise those who are. I suspect that after my mother, and other members of my immediate family, there is no other human group which has ministered more to my advantage and my pleasure than librarians. I am delighted that they have put up with my unspeakable promiscuity. I can think of few people who have books out of more libraries than I do. I hope I shall be encouraged and supported in this by the very great honor I have received today.

The impressive British Library Reading Room was planned by the architect Sydney Smirke and Anthony Panizzi, Keeper of Printed Books.

▼ ▼ ▼

**Further
Observations
by Lord
Anthony
Meredith
Quinton**

In the twentieth century a kind of consensus has developed that the essential, defining feature of the human species is language. Aristotle distinguished human beings from other animals in the light of their rationality. But although other animals are not argumentative and so do not go in for public displays of reasoning they are obviously, to varying degrees, intelligent. Marx defined the human species as the one that made tools, but that takes insufficient account of spider's webs and beaver's dams.

Language defines nationality which, despite its usually political surface, is at bottom a linguistic community; the collection of people we can most easily and effectively and comprehensively communicate with. With modern techniques of communication, it is perhaps the most important social thing about us, more important even than sex or age or social class.

Literature is the most authoritative and enduring deposit of language and it is the prime task of a national library to assemble and preserve as complete a collection of a nation's literature as it is possible to bring together. The language of mathematics and natural science is reasonably international; those of the humanities and imaginative writing are not. But humanistic scholars and, often in a less deliberate way, imaginative writers do take account of what is being written in the languages of large or neighboring nations. Also, in our energetically communicative world, nations are more than ever politically, economically, and culturally influenced by what is going on elsewhere. A national library's holding of its own literature has to be massively reinforced by the best of other nations' output if it is to serve the needs of scholars.

A national library of great wealth or, like the British Library, at least with a long and continuous history, will inevitably come to possess many things of primarily nonliterary interest: works valued because they are very old or physically beautiful or associated with historically interesting people or events. In my view a library is only incidentally or adventitiously a museum. If it has things of great nonliterary interest it should, of course, show them. But it should not, as I see it, assign a very high priority to the acquisition of material for the purpose of museum display.

It is to serve a wider public than the traditional scholarly elite, and I strongly believe it should, it will be the general public considered not as museum-goers, but as readers. Universal literacy is a comparatively recent achievement in the developed world. As it was emerging and in its earliest days it was applied to probably the world's greatest piece of literature: the Bible. Although its readers seldom had literary motives they generally benefited from its literary effect. There soon arose, of course, the industrial provision of escapist sub-literature and, at an even lower level, newspapers. And now there are the new easy alternatives to recreational reading: television and video.

Anyone who believes that humanity is in important respects at its best in its better books must favor the idea that libraries should act positively to encourage and assist reading and not just serve, at their various traditional levels of efficiency and comprehensiveness, to satisfy an existing want. Readers do not need simply assistance with the technicalities of consulting automated catalogues and of book-ordering; they need to be able to find out easily about the content and quality of books that exist about some subject they are interested in, be it historical novels about a particular neighborhood or a particular period, the history of some unobvious social institution like the hotel or the times of meals, comparative studies of the popular songs or ceremonial dress or courtship practices of different societies. For the inquiring mind a selective bibliography with brief, informative critical comment is one of the most valuable things in the world.

▼ ▼ ▼

It is to this kind of purpose that the Center for the Book at the Library of Congress is dedicated and I am firmly committed to the creation of something of the same sort in the British Library when it takes over its new, unified home at St Pancras.

In the middle ages literacy was confined to the clergy. It was enough to be literate, to be able to claim that important escape-route for misbehavers: Benefit of the Clergy. In due course Luther came along to proclaim the priesthood of all believers. What I am arguing for is a kind of Lutheranism of scholarship or, at any rate, the idea that many readers who are not scholars in the strict sense have a potentially scholarly interest in something. From the other direction, few scholars are scholarly about more than one thing. And unless, barbarously, they are interested in nothing but their scholarly specialism, they are nonscholars about most things in which they have some interest. In other words, all but the narrowest of specialists and those who do not read at all are general readers, uninformed or far from well-informed about what there is to read.

Present-day cataloguing techniques, which make possible retrieval of material about a given subject through keywords, can be enormously helpful for finding *what* there is, in all its qualitative variety. Human judgment is still needed to suggest what is, for various purposes and in various ways, worth reading. That is something ordinary scholars tend to be bad at. Out of nervous snobbery, they often ignore just those items directed to a nonexpert audience which would be most useful to a general reader. Library curators who have the scholarly skills, but are not under the same tiresome scholarship constraints, are admirably qualified to fill the gap. In that way, a national library will come to be not just a lake at which powerful beasts come to drink, but also a fountain from which animating streams flow out to shyer woodland creatures.

The convocation audience included members of the NYU community as well as distinguished leaders of the nation's libraries.

James H. Billington and Daniel J. Boorstin

on the

Library of Congress

The Library of Congress[2]

The Library of Congress was created by President John Adams in 1800 as a reference library for Congress, with $5,000 for the purchase of books and establishing an apartment to hold them. The library, housed in the Capitol, was destroyed when the British burned the Capitol in August 1814.

Within a month, former President Thomas Jefferson offered his personal library—considered one of the finest in

[2]From information provided by the Library of Congress.

The interior of the Library of Congress

The Library of Congress

the United States—as a replacement. After considerable debate, Congress accepted the offer and appropriated $23,950 for the collection of 6,487 additional books.

After two additional fires—a small one in 1825 and a serious one in 1851 that destroyed two-thirds of the holdings (including a substantial portion of Jefferson's gift), Congress voted money to replace the books and to construct rooms exclusively to house the collection.

In 1864, President Abraham Lincoln appointed Ainsworth Rand Spofford as Librarian of Congress. It was Spofford who opened the library to the public and expanded its collections. He successfully advocated a change in the copyright law so

The Main Reading Room's dome is 125 feet high and 100 feet wide

that the library received two free copies of every book, map, chart, dramatic or musical composition, engraving, cut, print, or photography submitted for copyright. A special agreement with the Smithsonian Institution resulted in the acquisition of scientific and foreign exchange materials. Spofford also arranged for the library to acquire the Congressional Record and all other U.S. statutes. He then used these to arrange document exchanges with all foreign nations with which the United States had diplomatic relations. To house the growing collection, he began a campaign for a new building.

In 1897, the Thomas Jefferson Building was completed under the supervision of Brigadier General Thomas Lincoln Casey, chief of the Army Engineers, and Bernard Richard Green, a civil engineer. The main reading room's dome, 125 feet high and 100 feet wide, was supported by marble columns and statues. In 1939, the John Adams Building was opened, and in 1980, the James Madison Memorial Building.

Among the libraries' greatest holdings are gifts from individual Americans. These include the Coolidge Auditorium and the creation of the Coolidge Foundation for the study and appreciation of music; the donation of Stradivarius instruments to be used for public performance; the Lessing J. Rosenwald collection of illustrated books and incunabula; Joseph Pennell's gift of Whistler drawings and letters; the private papers of Robert Todd Lincoln to his father, President Lincoln; and hundreds of thousands of letters and documents from famous individuals in politics, science, and the arts.

In addition, the library has many special items. The smallest book in the world, entitled *Ant*, is the size of an ant, 1.4 millimeters square. The Gutenberg Bible, purchased in 1930 along with 3,000 other volumes, for $1.5 million, is one of three perfect copies on vellum in the world. The earliest known motion picture, *Fred Ott's Sneeze*, was copyrighted by Thomas Edison in 1893 and is in the Motion Picture Division's collection. The library also owns the oldest example of print-

▼ ▼ ▼

Researchers using the Main Reading Room

ing in the world—passages from a Buddhist sutra printed in 770 A.D. The oldest written material in the library is a Sumerian cuneiform tablet dating from 2040 B.C.

The Library of Congress is the largest library in the world. It owns 84 million items and is visited by more than 2,000,000 people yearly. The library's computer system hold 12.5 million records and serves more than 3,000 terminals in the library and on Capitol Hill.

Presentation to Dr. James H. Billington

Convocation remarks by Dr. James H. Billington

44

▼ ▼ ▼

PRESENTATION TO JAMES H. BILLINGTON
by John Brademas

James H. Billington — Librarian of Congress, former Director of the Woodrow Wilson International Center for Scholars, historian, you bring to all your endeavors energy, breadth, and unshakable values. Valedictorian at Princeton and Rhodes Scholar at Oxford, you have made seminal contributions to the history of ideas, particularly in Russian studies. The Icon and the Axe, *your acclaimed interpretation of Russian culture, revealed a prodigious command of aesthetics, history, and religion even as your study,* Fire in the Minds of Men, *won praise for its vivid account of the European revolutionary faith. In your fourteen years at the Wilson Center, you built a lively crossroads for scholarly exchange, attracting thinkers and doers from all over the globe. You moved with ease to the helm of the world's largest national library, unique both for its collections in virtually all languages and disciplines and for its openness to all people. With characteristic grace, you said that as Librarian of Congress, your goal would be to bring "out that music that's already there."*

James H. Billington — "The pursuit of truth," you have asserted, "tends to keep us from the pursuit of each other." In light of the changes in the Soviet Union today, it is fortuitous that a person of your knowledge and experience should hold a post at the peak of American intellectual life. By virtue of the authority vested in me, I am delighted to confer upon you, my valued friend of nearly four decades, the degree of Doctor of Humane Letters, honoris causa.

▼ ▼ ▼

Dr. Daniel J. Boorstin, with his successor as Librarian of Congress, James H. Billington

Convocation Remarks by James H. Billington

Beginning the convocation program with me, in such company where I am the least experienced person on the platform, and a neophyte in view of the extraordinary experience that is in the audience, clearly reflects the influence of a certain school of Japanese flower arranging. This school argued that it was important to place a dead flower in the front of the arrangement, so that the flowers in the back would look even more glorious.

If the quest of scholarship in a dynamic society is to transform information into knowledge, as my distinguished

▼ ▼ ▼

predecessor Dan Boorstin has related it, and perhaps to distill knowledge into wisdom, the task of a democratic society is to bring wisdom into the ordinary life of its citizens. Each step depends on the preceding one: information is raw material; knowledge involves its selection and transmission in impersonal form. But wisdom is a quality that emerges slowly and resides in people — particularly in those who live with books and generate knowledge.

I would like to pay tribute, just as you have been kind enough to honor me today, to some of those people who live with, around, and for books as a way of saying thanks, and as a way of passing on the honors to those who really deserve it. The best way of expressing thanks for the honor accorded me here today is to pay tribute to some of those who mediated books to me — and in the process exposed me to at least some glimpses of wisdom.

My own father never had a formal education, but filled our house with used books which had a special value-added quality, if you like, for me — both because he had bought them and brought them back to us, and because they often contained the mysterious underlinings of the previous owner, which was in a way my introduction to scholarship — wondering why this passage rather than another had been singled out as important.

The wonderful émigré lady who first taught me Russian as a schoolboy during the war answered my question about why the Russians were doing so well at Stalingrad against the Germans by saying: "Read *War and Peace*." I always remember that advice, first of all because it made all books seem short to me, after that, and also because it indicated that the answer to an important question was often more likely to be found in yesterday's book than in today's newspaper.

I have learned two lessons about books over the years from my subsequent exposure to the field that began with *War and Peace*, the field of Russian culture. *One is the danger of deifying some books without giving freedom of access to others.* In a culture that has generally censored books and occasionally burned not just books thought to be subversive, but also those next to them on the shelves (that was Catherine the Great, not Stalin) — in such a culture, it is perhaps inevitable that exaggerated, even lurid, expectations should arise around a suppressed book as the secret bearer of some message of Utopian deliverance: from the old *golubinaia kniga,* or the "deep book" of the sectarians, right on to *Das Kapital* of the revolutionaries.

This has led to the selective, totemistic deification of some books and the total neglect of others, even today, in the U.S.S.R., where a few U.S. authors are published in enormous editions, but where there are almost no books — even in the best Soviet libraries — by representative U.S. authors explaining the social and historical contexts of the complex America in which the translated authors worked. A text without a context can become a pretext.

My second lesson is more hopeful. For I learned in long stretches of research in Russian libraries even before the age of *glasnot,* from the late 1950s to the early 1970s, before I became a bureaucrat, that libraries provided a quiet refuge for the scholarly integrity and the continued curiosity that can lead to wisdom, even under difficult conditions. Many of the finest scholars I have ever met were those who had simply retreated from the public arena and gladly accepted the comparative anonymity of library work, keeping alive in secret a heritage that could not be honored in public. I will always be grateful not just for their help and their bibliographical guidance, but for their example of dedication to learning. And what hope exists for the future there today is rooted in those who have lived among books. And the first steps of moral renewal in this age have been, indeed, the release of a series of long-suppressed books by Rybakov, Grossman, and the like.

And finally, as Librarian of Congress today, I worry about a very different problem, in our country, from the one of the

▼ ▼ ▼

country that I study—about how much we truly value and use the richness that we have in this and other of our great research libraries. Nearly three-fourths of the books in the Library of Congress are in foreign languages that Americans have generally ceased to study, and the great record of our own unique and inspiring national experience often seems neglected by our present-minded, video-oriented society.

"Exile is caused by forgetfulness and the secret of redemption is memory." So wrote Baal Shem-Tob, the founder of Hasidic Judaism. Librarians are the guardians of that memory; they are, as Carl Rochell has indicated, the link between the legacy of yesterday and the possibilities of tomorrow. In

Dr. James H. Billington and Dr. Daniel J. Boorstin after the convocation ceremony

The main catalog and reading room at the Library of Congress

▼ ▼ ▼

the information age in a democratic society, we will not be saved alone by the knowledge that is the province of the few. We will need the practical wisdom that can be shared with all and is the special province of those who live in, around, and for books. In the libraries of this land, and all the other ones throughout the civilized world, they will continue to play a major, if not the major, role in helping all our people recover memory and bring a measure of wisdom into their own lives. And I like to think that it is not those of us who are lucky enough to lead these great institutions, but to work in them and in the smaller and more immediately transmitting libraries of this nation and the rest of the civilized world, that New York University has honored at this convocation. I would like us all to join in giving them the thanks that is their due, for all the work that they have done.

NYU President John Brademas and Dr. Daniel J. Boorstin

Presentation to Dr. Daniel J. Boorstin

Convocation remarks by Dr. Daniel J. Boorstin

▼ ▼ ▼

PRESENTATION TO DANIEL J. BOORSTIN
by President John Brademas

Daniel J. Boorstin — historian and teacher, prolific writer, twelfth Librarian of Congress and Librarian of Congress Emeritus, you have throughout your several careers reveled in understanding the achievements of the human mind and in sharing that delight with others. Your own dazzling intellect propelled you, a Tulsa boy of fifteen, to Harvard, and, as a Rhodes Scholar, to Oxford. Our foremost social historian, you prefer the big topic and the broad view of it, tackling such themes as the Americanness of America and the chronicle of man's search for knowledge and thirst for creativity. Your wide-ranging and widely popular books have garnered many awards; the final volume of your trilogy, The Americans, *won the Pulitzer Prize for History. You combined erudition with imagination to transform the Library of Congress. On taking charge of that august institution, you vowed to "open it up"; and in a dozen years doubled the number of its users. You rebuilt and modernized our national library, with bold steps to preserve books and encourage reading; in a typically grand move, you initiated an inventory of what we have learned and what we do not yet know.*

Daniel J. Boorstin — you have said that the Library of Congress takes "all knowledge as its province and a whole nation for its audience," a description that could well fit you. I am pleased, by virtue of the authority vested in me, to confer upon you, a friend of many years, the degree of Doctor of Humane Letters, honoris causa.

▼ ▼ ▼

Convocation Remarks by Daniel J. Boorstin

In the beginning of my career as the Librarian of Congress, I had a curious problem. I felt myself fitting the description that Oscar Wilde once gave of a man who was pretending to be an impostor. I found myself, as a scholar, pretending that I was not really a librarian. But, in fact, all librarians are scholars, and all scholars must be librarians.

Perhaps over the years, living in Washington, D.C. has made me less sensitive to the pretensions of impostors. But I would like to say a few words about the mission of scholar-librarians and librarian-scholars. We are here today to celebrate scholarship, libraries, and librarians—the mystery and the paradox of freedom, of which libraries are the symbol.

We here celebrate the immortal word, the only inheritance of our past, of the whole human past, that remains untarnished in its original beauty.

We celebrate the paradox of freedom: That no word is sacred, but all words are sacred.

When we celebrate libraries, we celebrate a community. Books are the limbo and the link between a solitary person and humanity in community. Our hope and our delight were expressed by the Yeatses, father and son. John Butler Yeats said: "A work of art is the social act of a solitary man." So, too, is each work of literature. As the son, William Butler Yeats, remarked: "Though we cannot know the truth, we may embody it." That embodiment is our common treasure, of which libraries are the treasury. Our always-new world, the world of books.

NYU President John Brademas addresses the convocation audience

Vartan Gregorian
—on the—
New York
Public Library

This day crowns a work of National importance. The dedication of this beautiful structure for the spread of knowledge among the people. . . .

**The New
York Public
Library**

Since President William Howard Taft spoke these words at the opening of the New York Public Library in May 1911, more than one hundred million people have visited the landmark building at Fifth Avenue and 42nd Street, and consulted its preeminent research collection, encompassing fifty centuries of human thought and experience in three thousand languages and dialects.

Both grandeur and accessibility have come to characterize the library, whose

The main entrance to the Central Research Library of the New York Public Library

▼ ▼ ▼

meticulous design and construction required more than fourteen years. During this time, 1,500 sketches and drawings were rendered, and 530,000 cubic feet of marble were quarried to build the "people's palace." The foundations of the institution, however, were laid as far back as the end of the American Revolution.

During those early years, a young German immigrant, John Jacob Astor, arrived in the United States with only a few English pounds sterling. He built a sizable fortune as a fur trader, a tea merchant, and a speculator in New York real estate. Later, he turned his esteemed collection of 80,000 volumes into the Astor Library, which opened in 1854. Sixteen years later, retired merchant James S. Lenox formed the Lenox Library to house his prized collection of art, books, and manuscripts, including the first Gutenberg Bible brought to the United States.

DeWitt Wallace Periodicals Room, New York Public Library

Public Catalog Room, New York Public Library

Astor Hall (newly redecorated), New York Public Library

Public Catalog Room, New York Public Library

Astor Hall (newly redecorated), New York Public Library

▼ ▼ ▼

Though highly valued, these libraries were limited both in hours and in service to the public. An article in *The Nation* in 1880 decried: "Everyone knows that, for the general public, and particularly for the poorer portions of it, access to books is almost as completely cut off in this city as it is in the Adirondacks."

The potential for both a free and distinguished public library occurred when a third New Yorker, former governor and presidential candidate Samuel J. Tilden, set up a $5,000,000 trust for a "free library and reading room." Though

Main Reading Room, New York Public Library

▼▼▼

the bequest was contested by his relatives, $2,000,000 and 16,000 volumes from Tilden's own library were finally incorporated with the Astor and Lenox holdings in 1895 to create the New York Public Library. The City of New York then agreed to build and maintain "forever" the headquarters of this new, private institution, whose nucleus was the collections of Astor, Lenox, and Tilden.

The very name of the New York *Public* Library underscored that it was to be accessible and *free* (the nineteenth-century connotation of "public"). The actual operating budget of the library—acquiring, maintaining, and making accessible the vast collections—was and continues to be derived from

New York Public Library

The Celeste Bartos Forum is the place for lectures, concerts, and film presentations at the New York Public Library

private contributions from corporations, foundations, and individuals, and endowment income.

The centrally located Croton Reservoir was selected as the building site and the library's first director, John Shaw Billings, penciled an ingenious but controversial floor plan that was designed to serve readers quickly and efficiently. After an intense two-part competition among New York's leading architects, the commission was awarded to the firm of John Merven Carrere and Thomas Hastings, whose winning design followed Billings' interior plan and projected a Beaux-Arts style. At the time of its completion, *Harper's Monthly* wrote: "Few buildings in any period have been planned with greater patience and foresight, or have been executed with more technical painstaking or refinement."

▼ ▼ ▼

Once in operation, the library's accessibility and fast service were immediately noted as exemplary and prompted one journalist to contrast the old gentlemen of European libraries "shuffling about in felt slippers" with the "spry boys and girls" who served the reading public in America. In addition, anyone could enter the New York Public Library without question asked or paper signed, in contrast to the British Library, for example, which required an application endorsed by two householders of London.

Over the years, the number of visitors to the library increased and reached a peak of 4.5 million in 1934, when the library became the most popular of public institutions, and was lauded for its contribution to the sustaining of the country's morale during the years of unemployment. During this time, the stone lions that guard the library were nicknamed "Patience" and "Fortitude"—qualities needed to brave the Depression—by Mayor Fiorello LaGuardia.

The library continued to be open every single day of the year, including holidays, through the early 1960s, with only three exceptions: VJ Day in 1945; when a tugboat strike shut off oil deliveries in 1946, and on the day of the severe snowstorm in December 1960. Library hours were ultimately curtailed in the late 1960s and early 1970s because of the library's growing deficit. At the same time, endowment securities were sold rather than decrease annual acquisitions.

The library rebounded in the 1980s as the public and private sectors strengthened their partnership of financial support. Today, the library vivifies Ada Louise Huxtable's observation that it is "one of the last of the great nineteenth century buildings" which has "consistently filled twentieth century needs." The elegant ambiance of the building has been renewed as a result of a multimillion dollar restoration program, which incorporates state-of-the-art technology.

Major advances include the online computer catalogs that enhance the public's access to the library's vast resources. Temperature and humidity controls, crucial to preservation,

▼ ▼ ▼

have been installed in the eight levels of book stacks, and ground has been broken for stack expansion under Bryant Park to house the library's ever-growing collection. In addition, thousands of people now visit the library each year to see the art and literary exhibitions in the stately marble galleries, and to hear lectures and concerts in the skylit Forum.

Information and inspiration flow freely, and not just at the Fifth Avenue building. The library's research collections are housed at three other locations as well: the Library at Lincoln Center, the Schomburg Center for Research in Black Culture, and the Annex for newspapers and patents. And, it administers more than 80 Branch Libraries for the neighborhoods of Manhattan, the Bronx, and Staten Island.

These Branch Libraries, in turn, are depended on by more than five million people of all ages, not just for circulating and reference collections, but for such free cultural and educational events and services as literacy tutoring, microcomputer instruction, English language classes, job referral for the unemployed, and reading materials and devices for the disabled.

It would be impossible to imagine New York without the New York Public Library. As Calvin Trillin put it, "You don't have to enroll in anything, you don't have to buy a ticket to the balcony. . . . All you have to do is walk in here and this entire body of knowledge belongs to you."

New York Public Library

Presentation to Dr. Vartan Gregorian

Convocation remarks by Dr. Vartan Gregorian

66

▼ ▼ ▼

PRESENTATION TO VARTAN GREGORIAN
by John Brademas

Vartan Gregorian — as president of what you call the "people's university," you have revived the vast New York Public Library, with its four research and eighty-two branch libraries, as a visible and enduring monument to civilization. Respected teacher and historian, scholar and academic leader, you have returned the Central Research Library at Fifth Avenue and 42nd Street to its original splendor and you have demonstrated how a great library can contribute to the life and purposes of a great city. With extraordinary energy and tenacious optimism, you have won new friends and generated unprecedented support for the institution you lead. It is no wonder that "dynamic" and "magical" are words we associate with your success.

Vartan Gregorian — you once said, "The greatest threat to liberty is ignorance," and added, "The teacher in me will not give up." Like the stone lions, Patience and Fortitude, that majestically guard the beaux arts centerpiece of the New York Public Library, you have dedicated yourself to preserving our liberty by conquering our ignorance. I take much personal pleasure in conferring upon you, by virtue of the authority vested in me, the degree of Doctor of Humane Letters, *honoris causa.*

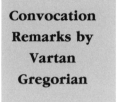

**Convocation
Remarks by
Vartan
Gregorian**

I accept this honor with gratitude and pride. I am grateful to New York University, its distinguished faculty, and its President, John Brademas. I am proud, for I accept this honor on behalf of the New York Public Library, the people's free university, and its 2,750 librarians and staff, for this recognition, in reality, belongs to them, not to me.

The libraries contain our nation's heritage, the heritage of humanity, the record of its triumphs and failures, the record of humanity's intellectual, scientific, and artistic achievements. The libraries represent humanity's collective memory. They are not repositories alone. They are instruments of civilization; they provide tools for learning, understanding, and progress. They are sources of information, yes, but they are also sources of knowledge, sources of wisdom, and sources of action. They are laboratories of human endeavor. They are windows to the future. They are sources of hope. They are sources of self-renewal. They are sources of self-determination, and autonomy, and, to use a new word, empowerment.

The libraries are the symbol of our community with humanity. They embody the spirit of humanity, a spirit which has been extolled throughout history by countless writers, scholars, philosophers, and artists. The library embodies a society's collective, but discriminatory memory. It is an act of honor to the past and a witness to the future, hence a visible judgment on both. The library is not only a diary of the human race, but marks an act of faith in the continuity of humanity.

This convocation is not one of celebration only, but rededication as well. Rededication to learning, and to knowledge; celebration of the human spirit, celebration of human dignity, intelligence, and will; celebration of tolerance, since the library is the only tolerant historical institution, where the right and the wrong, where the left and the right, where the Devil and God, where human follies and human endeavors, where

▼ ▼ ▼

Dr. Vartan Gregorian and Dean Carlton C. Rochell preparing for the convocation ceremony

human achievements and human failures—all of them are retained and classified in order to teach mankind what not to repeat, and what to try to emulate. The library is our house of intellect, our transcendental university, with one exception: no one graduates from a library. No one possibly can, and no one should. This convocation, in praise of libraries and librarians, is also a celebration of the librarians and the book, because the library is the center of the book, symbol of our identity, our historical identity, as my colleagues have so eloquently pointed out.

I have to thank Professor Fusi: he did not finish all of his quotation, leaving some for me; true gentlemanly Spaniard he is. So let me finish the quotation, one of the most eloquent

69

▼ ▼ ▼

quotations written about this subject. In the preface to the "Treasures of Spain" exhibit at the New York Public Library, Jorge Luis Borges wrote: "I believe books never disappear. It's impossible for it to happen. Of all mankind's diverse tools undoubtedly the most astonishing are the books. All the others are extensions of the body. The telephone is the extension of his voice. The telescope and the microscope extensions of his sight. The sword and the plow the extensions of his arms. In 'Caesar and Cleopatra,' when Bernard Shaw refers to the library of Alexandria, he says it's mankind's memory. I would say it's also mankind's imagination. Humanity's vigils have generated infinite pages of infinite books. Mankind owes all that we are to be to the written words. Books are the great memories of the centuries; consequently, their function is

Chancellor L. Jay Oliva and Dr. Vartan Gregorian

▼ ▼ ▼

irreplaceable. If books were to disappear, history would disappear. So would man." And, may I add, so would woman.

In conclusion, I must stress that we are not mere gatekeepers and doorkeepers of humanity's heritage. We also must protect its dissemination. We must beware of all censorship in whatever form it comes, because to censor, to tamper with truth, to tamper with our memory, is to commit a historical sin. We as librarians have a major duty, that we must all share all over the world, in order not to allow anybody to control, to twist, and most important of all, to manipulate our human will and through it our free institutions.

Further Observations by Vartan Gregorian

Libraries are as old as civilization. From the clay tablets of Babylonia to the computers of today, libraries stretch across more than five thousand years of humanity's insatiable desire to establish written immortality. The library is central to our free society. It is a critical element in the free exchange of information at the heart of our democracy.

Here, at the New York Public Library, though our institution is complex, our mission is simple and straightforward. The library's mission statement lays out our task quite clearly: "the New York Public Library is one of the cornerstones of the American tradition of equal opportunity. It provides free and open access to the accumulated wisdom of the world, without distinction as to income, religion, nationality, or other human condition. . . . It guarantees freedom of information and independence of thought. . . . It helps ensure the free trade in ideas and the right of dissent. . . . the New York Public Library's responsibility is to serve as a great storehouse of knowledge at the heart of one of the world's information centers, and function as an integral part of a fabric of information and learning that stretches across the nation and world."

Many burdens and challenges are inherent in running an institution as complex and sweeping as the New York Public Library. The Board of Trustees, administration, and librarians of this great institution work hard to remain true to our founding principles of the past at the same time that we strive to be responsive to the currents of the present and also remain dedicated to our readers of the future.

When circulating libraries were established in America in the nineteenth century, they were built primarily as a means to satisfy the educational needs of students and self-made people. Their tremendous growth and proliferation at that time reflected the ethic of self-improvement so pervasive in our society from the 1850s onward. Andrew Carnegie's far-seeing gift at the turn of the century, the establishment in New York of a pre-eminent noncirculating research source, surrounded by a constellation of branch libraries in the city's communities, is an extension of that concept. In the current absence of substantial cultural settings in our disadvantaged communities, the library today has assumed more responsibility than ever for mainstream social needs. In other ways, though, we have not changed. One of my greatest sources of pride as president of the New York Public Library is the continuance of the library's open, free, and democratic posture, the fact that we are here for Everyman, that we are indeed Everyman's university, the place where the scholar who is not college-affiliated can come and work and feel at home.

The New York Public Library has the least restrictive-use policy of any research library in the world, and the growth of socially conscious programs in its 82 branches complements that stance. The library must also be viewed through the larger context of being seen as a critical part of a vast and interlocking national network of research libraries. A part of a national system, it is in every library's interest to explore ways in which

▼ ▼ ▼

Dr. Vartan Gregorian greets Mrs. Elmer H. Bobst with Juan Pablo Fusi and André Miguel

collecting can become complementary. Shared collecting is essential to our survival.

While the library remains the house of the book, increasingly it is a home run by the computer. Here in the library, technology offers itself as both opportunity and problem. I personally often worry that the search for technological progress is no longer a means, but has become an end in itself, escaping from human control and thus dominating people, alienating us from ourselves, our society, and our environment. As far as the New York Public Library is concerned, we must remain aware that technology is a cultural artifact, something we have created. It is a tool, not a goal.

A major concern that faces all of us is who will have the right to access information during the information explosion

Restored Public Catalog Room, New York Public Library

▼ ▼ ▼

we now face? Those who do not gain access will remain ancillary to the learning process, rather than central to it; and we as librarians simply cannot allow this to happen. I am constantly reminding people that the amount of available information doubles every five years. On the other hand, the ratio of used to available information is decreasing all the time. Librarians and libraries must work to redefine their functions in the face of such unmitigating growth. Greater and greater burdens will be placed on libraries of the future to become expert selectors of information. They will have to make decisions with much greater discrimination if libraries are to persevere as true protectors of the culture. And I am concerned that the inevitable consequence in the library of the not-too-distant future will be that as institutions we will have to begin to pass along the costs of this information explosion to our users. The question then remains, how can we remain a free library for the use of all people, the people's university, in the face of this issue?

Another urgent and awesome problem facing libraries all over the world is the issue of the preservation of mankind's heritage. Millions of books, periodicals, manuscripts, and other material have already been lost, or at this very minute, are on the verge of extinction due to the ravages of time, pollution, use, misuse, and the very content of the paper itself. Almost everything published since the mid-nineteenth century has been printed on paper containing self-destructive acids. It is heavy irony indeed that the production of cheap paper—the instrument used to democratize the written word —also bore the seeds of its own destruction.

Our struggle for the preservation of endangered books, journals, periodicals, and papers is urgent and the problems we face are monumental. At the Library of Congress, at least five million volumes of its 20 million-volume book collection now crumble at the touch of a finger. Similar conditions prevail at the New York Public Library, Yale University Library, and other research libraries as well. The question of preservation of our nation's and humanity's record then demands a sound plan, effective national and international cooperation, a massive infusion of funds, and the introduction and utilization of new scientific and technological tools. Libraries, the federal, state, and local governments, and the publishing community must join hands to rescue the record of the past for the world of the future.

The need to reverse the tide of illiteracy is yet one more fundamental challenge that will also require a joining of forces. Twenty percent of adult men and women in our nation cannot read well enough to understand a want ad or write well enough to fill out a job application. The total number of these functional illiterates is estimated between 23 and 30 million. Some estimates put the annual economic cost at $224 billion, in the form of incompetent job performance, lost tax revenues, remedial education, welfare payments, and crime. Neither our economy, our democracy nor our society can afford such a waste.

As we approach the threshold of the twenty-first century, we must remind the public that libraries are not a frill or a luxury. Libraries are a part, a central part, of our free society. They are a critical component of the free exchange of information that is at the heart of our democracy. What will be the result of our political system when a majority of the people are ignorant of the ideals, traditions, and purposes of democracy? As Thomas Jefferson wrote: "A nation that expects to be ignorant and free expects what never was and never will be."